PLAYS AND PLAYLETS

By
VIRGINIA WHITMAN

MOODY PRESS
CHICAGO

CONTENTS

DAILY BREAD

Importance of Daily Bible Reading

Cast of Characters

Billy, *an older Junior boy*
Betty, *a younger Junior girl*
Mother
Father
Aunt
Grandfather

Setting: Living room of average American home

Scene: Billy *and* Betty *are on the floor reading the comics.*

        ❧   ❧   ❧

(Mother *thrusts her head in the door, back of them, and speaks.*)

Mother: Wouldn't this be a good time to do your daily Bible reading?

Betty: We can finish the funnies first, can't we? (Mother *exits before* girl *finishes speaking.*)

Billy (*scowling as he reaches for Bible*): These daily readings are a nuisance, if you ask me. I'm always having to stop doing something and read them.

Betty: But Billy, you know a person needs to read

the Bible. It tells him what to do. Besides, there are lots of interesting stories in it.

BILLY: I like the Bible all right, but it's bothering to read it every day that I don't like. Know what I'm going to do?

BETTY: No. What?

(*Without* BILLY *and* BETTY *noting it,* MOTHER *has reappeared in the doorway behind them, and is listening to their remarks.*)

BILLY: I'm going to read them for the whole week, right here and now. Then I'll be done with it.

(MOTHER *smiles and withdraws unobserved.* FATHER *and* AUNT *enter and pick up sections of Sunday paper and commence to read.* GRANDFATHER *enters with a letter in his hand. He is followed by* MOTHER.)

GRANDFATHER: How about running down to the corner and mailing my letter, children?

BETTY: I'll go. Billy's reading.

BILLY: I'm through. I'll go.

MOTHER: Both of you go, but come right back. Maybe we'll make some candy after a bit.

(BILLY *and* BETTY *express delight and depart noisily.*)

MOTHER (*to* FAMILY): Do you know what Billy was doing?

AUNT: Reading his Bible, the little dear. Wasn't that sweet?

MOTHER: But listen, he was reading *all* of his *daily* readings at one time.

FATHER: Doesn't he know what *daily* means?

MOTHER: When he comes back, I'm going to set him straight in an indirect way. You all take the cue from me and help out. Bring out the same idea in a different way.

FATHER: I don't know what you mean.

MOTHER: Just listen, and you'll catch on. Sh! Here they come.

(CHILDREN *enter breathlessly.*)

GRANDFATHER: You made a quick trip.

BETTY: Now can we make candy?

MOTHER: After a bit. I have to plan our next week's breakfasts first.

BILLY: Next week's? Why not just tomorrow's? A whole week would take too long. We want to make candy. Just plan tomorrow's today. And then tomorrow plan Tuesday's.

MOTHER: Oh, but I'm going to cook them all tomorrow.

BETTY: What for? They'd all get cold. I wouldn't like eggs on Friday that were cooked on Monday.

MOTHER: We'll just eat all of our breakfasts tomorrow morning, and then we'll be done with breakfast for the week.

BILLY: That sounds screwy to me. Even if we ate all our breakfasts in the morning, we'd have to have more food later in the week because we would have used up all our energy.

FATHER: I think that's a capital idea. I believe I'll follow the same plan with my police work. I'll detect all the crime this week, and then I can lay off the rest of the month.

BETTY: Daddy! You're joking. You can't arrest everybody *this* week. Some of them won't steal anything until *next* week. Then is when they'll have to be arrested.

AUNT: That gives me an idea too! I'll launder all the clothes we have tomorrow, and iron them the next day. Then I won't have to wash again this season.

BETTY: The clothes won't stay clean. What about the ones we get dirty?

BILLY: What *is* this? Some kind of a game? You all sound like a bunch of squares to me.

MOTHER: Watch out, boy. You started it.

BILLY (*plainly mystified*): *I* did?

BETTY (*giggling*): Oh, Billy! I bet I know. You said you were going to read all of your daily Bible readings at once.

BILLY (*getting a little annoyed*): And I did! So what?

MOTHER: The Bible is our spiritual food, Son. To be strong spiritually we need a portion of it each day, the same way we need breakfast every morning.

FATHER: And the Word of God convicts us of sin. As we read, we are arrested by what it says and made to realize that we're guilty of breaking God's laws. But we can't be convicted today of the sin we haven't yet committed.

BILLY: I see what you mean. Well, Auntie, you haven't had your say.

AUNT: As we read our Bibles, we find God's promises of forgiveness and cleansing. That too must be after we're conscious we are soiled by sin.

BETTY: So your idea wasn't such a bright one after all, Billy.

GRANDFATHER: Now wait a minute, all of you. Maybe Billy did get a mistaken idea, but he's not alone in it. Who is there of us that hasn't neglected on some days to look to God's Word for help and guidance?

MOTHER: You're right, Grandpa. I suppose every single one of us has been guilty at one time or another of neglecting our daily Bible readings.

AUNT: We should always think of them as necessary food for the day: spiritual food.

FATHER: And just as I buckle on my holster and gun every day when I report for duty, so we should have a weapon for the day's need—one taken from our Scripture arsenal.

BETTY: The Bible says the Word of God is the Sword of the Spirit. It calls it a hammer too.

GRANDFATHER: And a Christian needs his daily Bible reading the same as a carpenter needs his hammer.

MOTHER: If we think of all the things the Bible calls itself, we can see how important it is to our daily lives.

BETTY: What else does it call itself?

FATHER: Light, for one thing. (*Quotes Ps. 119: 105.*)

AUNT: Milk. (*Quotes I Peter 2:2.*)

BILLY: And meat, doesn't it?

MOTHER: Yes, and fire, and seed, and many other terms.

GRANDFATHER: I think we had better ask God to help all of us to turn to God's Word every single day and have a quiet time with Him of our very own, each one of us.

FATHER: You lead us in such a prayer, Grandpa.

BULWARK FOR THE FUTURE

Importance of Family Altar

CAST OF CHARACTERS

    FATHER
    MOTHER
    GRACE, *Junior girl*
    BOB, *Intermediate boy*
    JOHNNY, *an under-twenty serviceman in uniform*
    DICK, *serviceman*
    BUD, *serviceman*
    CHUCK, *serviceman*
    RAY, *serviceman*

SETTING: Arrange a curtain across the platform so as to divide it into two sections, both visible to the audience at the same time.

On one side provide a bunk bed and accessories to resemble a portion of a military barrack room. Hanging over the scene or on an easel to one side, have the caption, "When temptation came."

On the other side provide a living-room setting from an average American home. Above or to one side of it have the caption, "The memory that strengthened."

SCENE: (JOHNNY *enters barrack room and throws*

himself down on bunk as if depressed. DICK *enters and tosses a letter to him.*)

    ❧   ❧   ❧

DICK: Cheer up, Johnny. You got a letter from home after all. It got mixed up with my mail. (*He exits.*)

(JOHNNY's *face brightens as he sits up and opens letter. He reads aloud. As he is reading,* BOB, GRACE, FATHER, *and* MOTHER *slip quietly into their places in the living-room scene.* FATHER *picks up a Bible.*)

JOHNNY (*reading*): DEAR SON:

It was surely good to receive your letter and learn that you are getting along all right. It must be very interesting seeing those foreign places. Because the ways of the people are strange to you and their customs different, Satan might try to deceive you about what is right and wrong, but we shall be praying for you every day as we gather at our family altar. We love you so much, and expect great things for God from you, because you are His missionary in that particular place where you are now. . . .

(JOHNNY *shakes head negatively, and hides face in hands. Meanwhile, the four in the living room have fallen to their knees as in prayer.* FATHER *is speaking.*)

FATHER: Lord, we thank You for giving us these children. We pray that each will grow up to be a worthy witness for Thee.

MOTHER: Heavenly Father, I pray that if it is Thy

will to use Johnny in Thy service, that he may some time represent Thee as a missionary on foreign soil.

GRACE: Dear God, help Bob, and Johnny, and me to be true missionaries for You.

BOB: Dear God, if You think I could do the job, You may send me across the ocean to tell heathen people about You.

(DICK *has re-entered barrack room and addresses* JOHNNY *who lifts his face from his hands to listen.* FAMILY *at home unobtrusively rise from their knees during his conversation.*)

DICK: Hey, Johnny, a bunch of us are putting in for week-end passes to the big city. Want me to put your name down?

JOHNNY: Thanks, I'll let you know. It's swell of you to ask me.

DICK: There'll be bright lights and beautiful gals. (*Exits*)

(JOHNNY *drops his head into his hands as* FATHER *in other scene clears throat and opens Bible.*)

FATHER: Today our devotional reading is from Proverbs 5. You may not understand it very well now, but give attention and store it in your hearts. Sometime it may stand you in good stead.

(*He reads Prov. 5:1-8 in a clear voice. As he finishes,* BUD *enters the other scene, holding up a bottle.* JOHNNY *lifts his head.*)

BUD: Look, Johnny, what we got down at the village. It's the real stuff. Come on over to B room and have some.

JOHNNY: Thanks, Bud. You go ahead. Maybe I'll be along in a few minutes. I've got to shine my boots a bit. (*He reaches for equipment as Bud exits, then after a rub or two, he again buries his head in his hands. In home scene* MOTHER *has the Bible and is preparing to read.*)

MOTHER: Today's reading is from Proverbs 23:29-35. (*She reads those verses, also Proverbs 20:1.*)

(CHUCK *enters the other scene and* JOHNNY *looks up.*)

CHUCK: Listen, Johnny, you can't mope around in your bunk all the time. Let's take your cigarettes down to the black market and make a little spare cash. You've never drawn your allotment, and you could turn it into pure gold.

JOHNNY: Is that what the CO said?

CHUCK: Well, don't kid yourself. I'll bet he does it too.

(JOHNNY *shakes his head and* CHUCK *exits.* JOHNNY *sits quietly in thought. In home living-room scene,* FATHER *is handing Bible to* BOB.)

FATHER: Bob, you read for us today. The passage is Proverbs 1:10-15.

(BOB *reads it aloud. As he finishes it,* RAY *enters barrack room and begins motioning and talking excitedly.*)

RAY: After all these months of doing nothing, it looks like the fireworks are starting. I heard that the CO got word trouble has broken loose over the border, and that we'll probably see action in the next twenty-four hours. Come on down to the village with us, Johnny. Let's eat, drink, and be merry, for tomorrow we may die.

JOHNNY: Thanks, fella, but if that's the case I want to get a letter written.

(RAY *exits.* JOHNNY *gets out paper and starts writing. In home scene* MOTHER *speaks to* GRACE.)

MOTHER: It's your turn to read today, Gracie. It's from Psalm 27, verses 1-6. (GRACE *reads Ps. 27: 1-6.*)

FATHER: That's a good psalm to move into when anyone of us is in danger.

GRACE: What do you mean, Daddy? How could a person move into a psalm?

MOTHER: He means that you just believe every word of it, and tell God that you do, and that you're counting on Him.

(*Back in barrack scene* JOHNNY *is addressing an envelope. He picks up the page he has written, and folds it to go into the envelope. Then he unfolds it, speaking to himself as he does so.*)

JOHNNY: Let's see. Did I say all I meant to? (*He reads aloud.*)

DEAR MOM, DAD, BOB and GRACIE:

Just a few lines to tell you I've been thinking of you tonight, especially of the times we used to be together in the living room for our daily devotions.

Maybe I didn't always seem like I was paying attention. Maybe there were times I acted fidgety, and as if I wished it were over, but believe me, I'm glad now we had it, because it has been a bulwark to me many a time. In fact, I'm surprised at how many Scripture passages I remember, and the comments you made, and the prayers that were offered. I wish some of my buddies here had had a family altar at home.

The scuttlebutt is that we might see action tomorrow. One of those border disputes has flared up, according to rumor. So I don't know what the future holds, but as our pastor used to say, I know who holds the future.

And if the Lord permits me to live and do so, I want to try harder to be a witness for Him—one who is worthy of the name. So far, I haven't been very out and out as a witness, more of a secret disciple of Christ. Please pray on in the family circle that I'll be stronger and have more courage to give an open testimony, especially that my life will show on whose side I am.

Mother wrote in her letter which came today about me being a missionary in this place. It made me realize that maybe this is the answer to those prayers we used to pray at family altar. I love you all.

(*While he has been reading, the home family are on their knees.* JOHNNY *puts the letter into the envelope, licks the flap, and then he drops to his knees.*)

I HAD A BAD DREAM

Importance of Memorizing Scripture

CAST OF CHARACTERS

RUTH, *teen-age girl*
ROY, *teen-age boy*
LILA, *teen-age girl*
HERB, *teen-age boy*
ELEANOR, *teen-age girl*
BILL, *teen-age boy*
LEADER, *adult*

SETTING: A church social

SCENE: GROUP *is seated in a semicircle at center of stage with* LEADER *at one end. He stands to speak.*

       ✖   ✖   ✖

LEADER: Our last game this evening is, "I Had a Bad Dream." Each of you must tell about an incident in which you were in some critical situation and found, to your chagrin, that you lacked some essential item. You must not name the item, but must end your account with some phrase such as, "I reached for my .... and didn't have it." After all have related their stories, we'll vote on the best one.

RUTH: I dreamed I had boarded a space ship for

Mars. It was a big circular one, lined around its circumference with good-looking guys and nice old ladies. I was dressed up fit to kill, and I had a lot of luggage and was carrying a beautiful purse. I opened it to take out my . . . . and didn't have it.

GROUP: Money? Compact? Identification? Passport?

RUTH: No. My ticket.

BILL: But you have to present your ticket before you board a plane.

RUTH: Oh, well, this was a space ship and it was a dream.

LEADER: Let's hear from the next storyteller.

ROY: I dreamed I was cashier in a bank. The president had just been by and bragged about how valuable I was to the bank because of my charming personality, good looks, reliability, honesty, and everything. Ahem! I was sailing around on a rose-colored cloud, imagining I'd get a notice I'd been promoted to third vice-president when I felt something cold pressed on the back of my neck, and a voice said, "Hand over the cash." I had no choice but to do so. Then adhesive tape was pasted over my eyes and mouth, and I was bound hand and foot to a chair with cords. After a long struggle I got my right hand loose and wriggled it down into my pocket to get my . . . . but it wasn't there.

GROUP: Gun? Keys? Knife?

ROY: That's it. My knife.

BILL: You've been watching TV. That was a good yarn.

LILA: I dreamed I was coming home late from working overtime, and suddenly I realized I was being followed. If I hurried my steps, those behind me picked up. If I slowed down, they slowed down. Finally I came to a real dark place, and I began to run. So did the one behind me, and I could hear him coming faster and overtaking me. I felt a hand closing around my throat. I tried to get my .... but I didn't have any.

GROUP: Gun? Knife? Flashlight?

LILA: No. My voice. I was so scared I couldn't even gurgle.

LEADER: Very clever. Now the next one.

HERB: I don't dream. I just go to sleep and snore. You'll have to pass me.

BILL: Aw, go on, be a sport.

HERB: I told you I don't dream.

LEADER: O.K. Let's hear the next one.

ELEANOR: I dreamed I was aboard a big air liner bound for Hawaii. It was night and everyone was asleep. The stewardess turned on all the lights and said, "We've developed engine trouble, and are going to have to ditch. You will have enough time to get out, and everyone should make it all right because there are several ships in our immediate vicinity to pick us up. Please listen carefully to my instructions and follow them exactly."

We did, but the plane had too much gas yet, and

had to circle 'round and 'round to use up more of it. Everyone was taking it calmly except a girl in the seat beside me. She began to cry. She wasn't making a noise, but I could see the tears falling down her cheeks.

"Don't cry," I whispered, "everything's going to be all right."

(*Teller of tale is very convincing and dramatic, and* PLAYERS *all become tense and sober.*)

"I'm afraid," the girl confessed. "I've done some terribly wrong things in my short life, and now I know we're going to die and I'm not ready. I'm a sinner. I'm not ready to meet my Maker."

"But you can be ready," I told her, "all you have to do is repent and believe—."

"Believe what?" she wept, water running from her eyes and nose.

"Believe—." I paused to give her a .... and I didn't have any. I'd forgotten them all."

GROUP: Kleenex? Handkerchief? Tranquilizer?

ELEANOR: No none of them.

BILL: What?

ELEANOR: Scripture verse.

GROUP: (*sort of let down*): Oh!

ELEANOR: Folks, wouldn't it be terrible if something like that happened? Suppose you were with a lost person in a perilous situation and you couldn't think of a Scripture text on salvation.

HERB: I'll have to confess I don't know a single one.

LILA: I don't know very many.

ROY: Neither do I.

RUTH: (*trying to speak lightly*): Oh, well, don't the Gideons put Bibles on all the air liners now?

LEADER: I don't know about that, but I can think of a lot of places where there wouldn't be a Bible.

HERB: Like the bottom of a cliff.

LILA: Or pinned under the wreckage of a car.

ROY: Or floating around in a life preserver.

LEADER: There's just one sure place to have the Word of God, and that's in your heart through memorizing it.

ELEANOR: It's time to go home, and I've got to be on my way, but believe me, before I go to sleep tonight, I'm going to memorize at least one text. My dream woke me up!

LEADER: By next week we should decide which was the best.

THE LORD SAID SING

Importance of Choir Service

CAST OF CHARACTERS
  MR. BROWN, *choir member*
  MRS. CLARK, *choir member*
  MISS COLES, *choir member*
  MR. RUNYAN, *choir member*
  MR. JOHNSON, *choir member*
  MISS MOORE, *choir member* (*younger*)
  DIRECTOR
  REPORTER
  Four more choir members

SETTING: Choir area of a church

SCENE: DIRECTOR *is conducting choir rehearsal when approached by a young newspaper* REPORTER.

      🙖   🙖   🙖

REPORTER: Pardon me for interrupting, but I was sent out by the editor of the *News* to get a story on the special program of music you are preparing.

DIRECTOR: (*motioning* CHOIR *to be seated*): Certainly. What would you like to know?

REPORTER: When, where, what, how many voices, soloists, and so on.

DIRECTOR: You'll find all of that on these printed

programs. (*Hands him one.*) Is there anything else
you would like to know?

REPORTER: Yes. I'd like to know why these members are giving their time, free I understand, to come
here and practice. Why do you do it? (*He addresses last remark to* CHOIR.)

DIRECTOR: Who would like to answer?

MR. BROWN (*rising*): The Bible says we should
use our talent, whatever it is, for Him. There are
many things I can't do. I'm too poor at figures to
make a secretary or treasurer, too slow a thinker
to make a teacher, too bashful to be an usher, but
I can do well enough to sing bass in the choir. I
use my one ability in that way.

MRS. CLARK: (*rising as man sits down*): I'm about
like Mr. Brown only I can't even sing very well. But
here in the choir I get training. The experience and
practice are profitable to me.

MISS COLES: (*rising*): I think music, properly
rendered, adds to the services. If sung as unto the
Lord, it gives reverence, dignity, and beauty to the
worship of the Lord. That's why I help out in the
choir.

MR. RUNYAN (*rising*): I think music extends the
church's ministry beyond its walls. People who never
enter a church may pass by and get a message from
God just by hearing us sing.

MR. JOHNSON: (*rising*): Inside or outside of the
church, there may be persons who fail to heed, or
shrug off, the spoken word, but who can be reached

by a message in music. That's always my prayer, when I sing.

MISS MOORE (*rising*): Well, according to my Bible, the Lord said, Sing, so I just sing!

DIRECTOR (*addressing* REPORTER): Have these remarks helped?

REPORTER: I should say so, more than you'd guess. You see, my mother and pastor have both urged me to join the choir, and I couldn't see it. But these testimonies have been very convincing. The speakers seem so sincere and happy about their singing. I'm convicted I owe the Lord my singing service.

DIRECTOR: Let me add my testimony. The Bible says, "Let the redeemed of the Lord say so." If you've been saved by faith in Christ as a personal Saviour, why not say so, and say it in song? Let's all sing, "Saved, Saved, Saved!" Can you join us?

(REPORTER *joins in as all sing.*)

DOES ANYONE CARE?

Importance of Evangelism

CAST OF CHARACTERS
> MR. KING, *husband*
> MRS. KING, *wife*
> MR. LEE, *unseen radio announcer*

SETTING: Breakfast table of average American home. Have an easel at side of stage on which days of week are successively displayed as noted.

SCENE: MR. and MRS. KING *are seated at breakfast table. Mr. King is reading newspaper and sipping coffee.* MRS. KING *is eating a roll.*

❧ ❧ ❧

MONDAY

MR. KING: I see there's been the worst fire in the history of Missouri. St. Joseph[1] and all its suburbs have been swept by fire; everything and everybody are burned to a crisp.

MRS. KING: For goodness sake! (*Pauses to bite roll.*) What's the weather report for today? Is it going to be a good washday?

[1] Names of cities of like population but nearer to the place of dramatization may be substituted for those used in this script.

23

TUESDAY

MR. KING: It says a bad tornado hit Topeka, Kansas.[1] Killed all the people in Topeka, and half of the rest of the county.

MRS. KING: Can you imagine that! (*Pauses to bite roll.*) I've got a big ironing to do this morning. I hope I can get it done by noon.

WEDNESDAY

MR. KING: There's been a flood in Arkansas. Swept over Little Rock[1] and drowned a majority of the residents.

MRS. KING Must have been a lot of water. (*Pauses to bite roll.*) Don't forget to leave the car for me. You know I'm going to that luncheon.

THURSDAY

MR. KING: They had a big explosion at Cedar Rapids, Iowa,[1] yesterday. It wiped out the entire population.

MRS. KING: Iowa is one state I've never visited. (*Pauses to bite roll.*) We have missionary circle meeting at the church this afternoon.

FRIDAY

MR. KING: Did you hear or feel anything last night? The paper says there was an earthquake in our part of the state. A big crack opened up in the ground and swallowed Springfield[1] and all of Greene County.

MRS. KING: That's odd. I didn't feel a thing. I slept like a log. (*Yawns.*) But then I was tired. I surely don't feel much like house cleaning today.

MR. KING: (*switching on radio*): Let's get the news report and see if anyone we knew was involved. (*Pause*) What's the matter? I can't get Springfield.'

MRS. KING: Naturally not. What have you there?

MR. KING: It's probably that morning devotions fellow from Centerville.

MR. LEE: "Yes, friends, every fifteen minutes in yonder heavenly world the news is proclaimed that a thousand souls have gone into eternity without hope and without God. Every morning in Heaven it may be reported that a city larger than Lincoln, Nebraska, has been utterly wiped out, gone into eternity."² Do you care? If so, what are you doing about it? (*Voice fades on last statement.*)

MRS. KING: Well, I don't have time today to do anything. I'm cleaning house.

MR. KING: Nor do I. I've got to be on my way to work. (*Both arise and start off stage.*)

MRS. KING: We've got all we can do tending to our own affairs.

MR. LEE (*speaking louder*): "And take heed to yourselves, lest at any time your hearts be overcharged with surfeiting, and drunkenness, and cares of this life, and so that day come upon you unawares—Luke 21:34."

'This quotation appeared in a publication of the Back-to-the-Bible Broadcast.

(MR. and MRS. KING *exit without seeming to heed as* MR. LEE *continues.*)

MR. LEE: Friends, you who claim to be Christ's are not as apt to become negligent about the lost because of drunkenness and the like, as you are because of the cares of this life. You will arise each day, absorbed with thoughts of your job, your livelihood, your housekeeping, your social engagements, yes, even your church meetings, and give no thought or have any concern or burden for the thousands of lost ones who slip into eternity moment by moment. May God convict us of our guilt!

(*Hymn "Is It Nothing to You?" may be rendered as if concluding the radio broadcast.*)

What can you do to help
see that the lost and dying
souls have the printed word
of God ready for them

EACH ONE WIN ONE

Methods of Personal Evangelism

CAST OF CHARACTERS

ETHEL, *an eager young woman*
DON, *an earnest young man*
NARRATOR, *an older man*

SETTING: No particular background required. A set of placards is the only property needed.

SCENE: NARRATOR *stands before audience and reads Romans 12:1, 2. Then addresses audience.*

       ❧   ❧   ❧

NARRATOR: Who is ready to respond to this plea?
(DON and ETHEL *step forward from separate spots in the audience. They mount the platform where the narrator shakes hands with them.*)

NARRATOR: What would you like to do for your Lord and Master?

ETHEL and DON: Save souls!

NARRATOR: How do you propose to go about it?

DON: I'd like to be a preacher, and if the Lord dared bless me with such an evangelistic ministry, I'd like to see thousands walk the aisles for Christ every week.

ETHEL: I couldn't exercise a ministry like that, but I do want to be a soul-winner. If I became skilled in personal witnessing, maybe I could deal with individuals in such a way as to bring them to Christ. I know my ambitions look small compared with his, but if I could win a couple of souls a year to Christ and be the means of their becoming soul-winners in turn, I would thank God.

NARRATOR: According to thy faith be it unto thee. Come back in six months and report to me.

(NARRATOR *quotes Dan. 12:3 as couple return.*)

DON (*jubilantly*): My cup runneth over! The Lord has indeed mightily blessed me. For the past six months I have seen 1,000 persons genuinely converted each week. This is my report, praise His name! (*Displays placard bearing numerals 26,000.*)

ETHEL (*modestly*): I have nothing spectacular to offer. Soon after I left you I led one soul to Christ and she was such a babe in Christ she seemed to need a great deal of nurturing in His Word so I devoted myself to training her in what I knew. And she learned! She too won a soul to Christ. But these two are all I can trace to my ministry. (*Displays placard bearing numeral 2.*)

NARRATOR: Go back and continue your ministry. Young man, pray God to give you humility to bear the blessing He is pouring out on you. Continue to preach the Gospel in all the power with which God endues you. But do not disdain her ministry. Each is needed. Pray for one another.

Young woman, go win some other soul to Christ, and each time you win one, train her and bid her in turn to win someone else to Christ. Form a chain of believers. Come back at the end of the year and report again. (*They depart.*)

(NARRATOR *quotes II Tim. 2:2 as couple return.*)

DON: Again I come rejoicing. God hath done great things whereof we are glad. I have maintained my goal of 1,000 souls a week. This is my report to date, praise His name! (*Holds up placard bearing numerals 52,000.*)

ETHEL: My experience is just as before. My total to date is only four souls. (*Displays placard bearing numeral 4.*)

NARRATOR: Go out again and continue your soul-winning efforts. Keep up the program you have begun and report back in three years. (*They depart. NARRATOR quotes Ps. 126:6 as couple returns.*)

DON: I am back as you instructed. My average has been maintained, 1,000 souls a week. Here is my report. (*Holds up placard saying 156,000.*)

ETHEL: Here am I too. My converts and I have not labored in vain, but our results are so small compared with his. Here is our report. (*Displays placard numbered 64.*)

NARRATOR: Come back in two years. Let us see what fruit a total of five years of labor shall have produced. (*They depart.*)

(NARRATOR *quotes I Cor. 15:58 as couple returns.*)

Don: My God continues to bless me. Here is the report on five years of labor. (*Displays placard numbered 260,000.*)

Ethel: How insignificant my returns seem, but this is the five-year record of my "each one win one" effort. (*Displays card numbered 1,024.*)

Narrator: The time is short. Renew your efforts. Do not pause to return until another five years have elapsed. Then we shall see what ten years of service in His name has netted. (*They depart.*)

(Narrator *quotes II Tim. 4:2 as couple return.*)

Don: It indeed thrills my soul to be able to report a full 520,000 won to Christ through my preaching of His Word! (*Displays placard numbered 520,-000.*)

Ethel: But surely there is some mistake. Don't you mean 520 million?

Don: No, 1,000 a week for ten years is 520,000.

Ethel: But we—here is our report—(*Displays placard numbered 1,048,576.*)

Narrator: To God be the glory! Come back in another five and one-half years. (*They depart.*)

(Narrator *quotes I Cor. 3:6, 7 as they return.*)

Narrator: Fifteen and one-half years since they first came. I wonder what report they will bring.

Don: I grow weary in the work, but God has not failed me. I have kept the faith. Here is the report. (*Displays placard numbered 806,000.*)

Ethel: I do not wish to displease you, but I have been unable to keep the record. All I and my converts know is that we cannot seem to find any more souls to win until some more have reached the age of accountability. The world's entire present population has been reached and won to Him.

NARRATOR: Well done, thou good and faithful servants; enter thou into the joy of the Lord. Each of you has been a worthy witness. Not all, my dear man of God, can be used of God to win 1,000 souls a week, but certainly it was God's plan for each one to win one.

Note: *The above is based on an article which originally appeared in* MOODY MONTHLY *from which statistics were lifted. If a longer and more elaborate program is desired, an appropriate song could be rendered each time the couple departs. During its rendition they could change costumes and be made to appear more mature as the years presumably pass.*

IN A BUS STATION

Methods of Personal Evangelism

CAST OF CHARACTERS

SUE, a young woman
HELEN, *a young woman*

SCENE: SUE *is seated in waiting room of a bus station, reading her Bible. Looks up and recognizes a traveler carrying luggage about to pass her.*

❧ ❧ ❧

SUE: Well, Helen Jones, of all people! What are you doing here? Hasn't it been simply ages since we last met? Do sit down a minute.

HELEN: Thanks. I'm traveling for the Federated Culture Club. It's so fascinating! You meet so many people who really are somebody, and it broadens one's view so too. But what are you doing? Certainly not reading the Bible! Did some of your family just die?

SUE: Of course not! Why not read the Bible?

HELEN: Why not, indeed! With all my recollections of the wicked imp you were in our schooldays.

SUE: Remember the times we raided the icebox after 9:30?

HELEN: And the time we got campused for the week end?

SUE: Have you gained any more dignity with the years?

HELEN: Just on state occasions. Underneath, I'm the same old bad egg I always was, and you know that was pretty bad.

SUE: Bad enough to be lost, Helen?

HELEN: Why, Sue, what do you mean? You know I never did anything *really* bad or wrong.

SUE: Oh, you aren't a sinner?

HELEN: A sinner! Why, I don't do anything worse than everybody else does. I don't mean I'm an angel, but I'm as good as anyone else.

SUE: There's nothing to get indignant about, Helen. Only it's a shame that Christ's coming means nothing to you.

HELEN: What do you mean, Sue?

SUE: (*Quotes Luke 5:31, 32.*)

HELEN: Well, I may not be righteous; I said I wasn't perfect, but certainly I'm not the ungodly sinner you try to make me out to be.

SUE: But that's the ones Christ died for. (*Quotes Rom. 5:6, 8.*)

HELEN: Well, Sue, I can't understand you. To hear you talk anyone would think I was a street woman or someone of that type. Are you trying to insult me?

SUE: Of course not, Helen, dear. I'm just as great a sinner as you are. We have all sinned. The Bible says so. (*Quotes Rom. 3:23.*)

HELEN: Yes, but as I said before, I'm not a thief

or a murderer or a drunkard. Why should I go to Hell?

SUE: That isn't the reason people go to Hell. Let's see what God says about why we're condemned. Look here in John 3 (*reads substituting, "Is condemned already because he's a liar, a thief, and a drunkard"*). Is that what it says, Helen?

HELEN: No, it says, "Because he hath not believed on the name of the only begotten Son of God." But I don't reject Christ. I believe in Him.

SUE: How do you believe in Him? Just as a great Example, a Good Man, a Bible Character, or as the One who saved you from everlasting punishment by taking your place and bearing your sins for you?

HELEN: But why should I be everlastingly punished? How am I such a great sinner?

SUE: Helen if you found that you had committed the first and great sin, would you believe you are lost, condemned, and in need of a Saviour?

HELEN: Why, of course, but I told you I've never—.

SUE: Look here at Matthew 22:35 (*reads*). If that is the first and great command, what would be the first and great sin?

HELEN (*slowly*): Well—I suppose to break the first and great command.

SUE: Have you kept it? Have you always loved God with *all* your heart, and with *all* your soul, and with *all* your mind?

HELEN: I'm afraid not.

SUE: That's the point. None of us has. So we all need a Saviour, and Christ is that Saviour. Helen, if you would accept Him as your Saviour and Sovereign you would have a peace and joy and richness in your life that you have never experienced before. There is nothing like it. Won't you do so?

HELEN: I never had it explained to me like this before. I—.

SUE: They're calling my bus. I'm going to visit my married sister. I've got to go, but I shall be praying that you will accept the Lord Jesus Christ as your own personal Saviour and be born into the family of God without further delay. Don't put it off. Do it now. 'By!

CALL ON AN ABSENTEE

A Wrong Method of Visitation

CAST OF CHARACTERS

BARBARA, *teen-age girl in wraps*
KAREN, *teen-age girl in wraps*
MILDRED, *teen-age girl*

SETTING: Sidewalk in front of a doorway.

SCENE: BARBARA *and* KAREN *meet in front of doorway.*

❧   ❧   ❧

BARBARA: My! I'm glad to see you. I was just wishing I could find someone to make this Sunday school class call with me. I promised Sandra I'd go, so we'd be 100% in visitation this week.

KAREN: I can't go now. It's dinnertime and I'm simply starved. Who is it you have to see?

BARBARA: Mildred Bates. She lives right here. It won't do a bit of good to see her. I wish she'd join another church, move away, or do something so we could get her off the roll.

KAREN: Maybe she won't be home.

BARBARA: We might get a break like that. Come on, we'll knock just once, and if no one hears us we'll write "No response" on the report slip and it'll count for a call just the same.

(*They knock, and the door immediately opens.*)

BARBARA: Hello, Mildred. How's everything?

MILDRED (*coolly*): I think I'll live.

KAREN: You haven't really been sick, have you?

MILDRED (*tartly*): Oh, no, I just thought I'd room at the hospital awhile, but one of the interns got funny and took out my appendix when I wasn't looking.

BARBARA: Not really? Why didn't you tell us?

KAREN: I don't think even the teacher knew it. How long has it been since you were in class?

MILDRED: I was there Easter.

BARBARA: Wanted to show your new hat, I bet. Say, then you haven't heard the latest news. Did you know about the fight between our teacher and the class president?

MILDRED: Again? You'll have to spare the details, I have a date.

KAREN: So have I. We must run on.

BARBARA: Take care of yourself, Mildred. You don't want to get adhesions. (*Door closes and they turn away.*)

KAREN: I wonder whom she's dating?

BARBARA: It's hard telling. Say, do you know we forgot to ask her to come to Sunday school?

POINTS FOR DISCUSSION IF DESIRED:

What errors were committed?

Wrong motive for call

Evidently not preceded by prayer

Not interested in absentee personally
Not informed about circumstances of absence
Chose poor time, dinner hour
Repeated gossip
Nothing accomplished

CALL ON A PROSPECT

A Right Method of Visitation

CAST OF CHARACTERS

JIM STANLEY, *a young man in wraps*
DICK TUCKER, *a young man in wraps*
TED MATHEWS, *a young man*

SETTING: Sidewalk in front of a doorway

SCENE: JIM *and* DICK *are walking along engaged in conversation. They have Bibles under their arms, and one is consulting a notebook.*

        ∾   ∾   ∾

JIM: That was a helpful prayer Mr. Trent offered. I always feel better prepared to make a call when there has been prayer about it.

DICK: I certainly am anxious for us to enlist some of our census prospects. Now this one (*consulting a card*) is Ted Mathews, age 21, member of a church in Texas.

(*They pause and knock.* TED *answers.*)

JIM: How do you do? Are you Ted Mathews? (*Man nods.*) I'm Jim Stanley and this is Dick Tucker from the Bethel Church down at the corner of Main and Lincoln. We came to invite you to our young people's department of the Sunday school. We have a jolly group of young men and women, and would like you to come down and get acquainted.

TED: Thanks. I may do that some time. I usually have something to keep me busy on Sunday morning, like putting new rings in my car, and—.

DICK: There is always plenty to do, all right, but we'd surely like to have you come over and help us along. I understand you hold membership in one of our Texas churches. Did you have an office in the young people's department of your Sunday school?

TED: I used to be president of my class, and sometimes I led the singing in the department, but to tell the truth I've never got started in Sunday school since coming here. That's been more than a year ago, but you know how it is with a new job, in a strange place, and so on.

JIM: Say, if you'd come to Sunday school once, you wouldn't be strange any more, and with your experience you could help us a lot.

TED: You had better say you could be a lot of help to me. I've just about turned heathen, I guess. My mother writes every once in awhile and asks me if I enjoyed the lesson Sunday, or something like that, and I wouldn't even know what the subject was.

DICK: The class you'd be in has a dandy teacher. He surely makes Bible study interesting, and he's a swell fellow too.

JIM: And there's a lot of regular guys in the class too. You'd like them. Can't you come this Sunday?

DICK: How about my coming by for you?

TED: That won't be necessary, thanks. And I'll think it over.

DICK: Try and get there at 9:30 because the superintendent has promised a special surprise feature in the opening program.

JIM: And bring your Bible if you have one, because you'll get more out of the study. By the way, the lesson is found in Acts 4 if you should want to take a look at it.

DICK: We're surely glad we met you.

JIM: Yes, and we'll be on hand to make you acquainted on Sunday morning.

TED: Thanks for coming. I'll try to be there.

POINTS FOR DISCUSSION IF DESIRED:

What appeals did the visitors use? (Social fellowship, good Bible teaching, curiosity. We need you. You need us.) What information did they secure? (Previous experience, spiritual attitude, family background, employment, car ownership.) What information did they dispense? (Time of opening, lesson location, teacher, class, program.)

What were some commendable features of this visit? (Preceded by prayer, planned, interested in the individual, tactful, friendly, invited him to Sunday school rather than just to their class.)

THE SHORT-WAVE BAND TO HEAVEN

Principles of Prayer

CAST OF CHARACTERS

TIM, *a young man about twenty years of age*
MRS. LAKE, *his mother*

SETTING: The living room of a modest American home, one corner of which is fitted up with desk and short-wave radio equipment.

SCENE: TIM *is seated at desk with earphones on head. MOTHER is reading Bible when scene opens, but lays it aside and takes up mending, or some other handwork.*

❧ ❧ ❧

TIM (*talking into radio*): Listen, Jake, did you hear that police dispatcher awhile ago? I thought I'd split. He said, "Car number 9 report to 850 Valley, bull-dog has man in pajamas treed." (*Chuckles and pauses as if listening.*) Yeah, the officer reported back that the man had stopped out in his pajamas to get the morning paper and the door slammed shut, locking him out. He started into the neighbor's to telephone his wife, and the dog mistook him for a prowler. Lady across the street saw his predicament and phoned the police. (*Pauses again.*) Yeah, I listen to them a lot, get a big kick out of some of the calls. O.K. Be talking to you again. This is UBYS signing off. (*He takes off headphones and lays them on desk.*)

The mail ought to be here by now. I hope I have a letter telling me to come in for an interview on that job.

(*He exits,* Mrs. Lake *bows head as if praying.* Tim *re-enters and throws down a paper and magazine.* Mrs. Lake *looks up.*)

Tim (*pacing floor nervously*): Not a single letter! What am I going to do, Mom? I've got to have work, and I've tried *everything*.

Mrs. Lake: Everything? Have you tried God? Have you really talked to Him about your situation?

Tim: Now, Mom, that's all right for you, but you can't expect me to pray about affairs in *my* life.

Mrs. Lake: Why not? You've trusted Christ as your Saviour. God is your heavenly Father. Why not consult Him about your affairs the same as you do your earthly father?

Tim: Oh, but I can *see* Dad, while in praying you're just sounding off into space.

Mrs. Lake: It could look like that was all you were doing when you talk over your short-wave set, just sounding off into space—.

Tim: But someone answers my CQ. I get a response. Besides, sometimes they call me instead of me calling them.

MRS. LAKE: Properly understood, the principle of prayer is the same. Prayer is two-way communication too.

TIM: I don't see how.

MRS. LAKE: That is a point you and a lot of other believers overlook. God is equipped, if I may reverently put it that way, for broadcasting as well as receiving. But many of us are so self-centered that we have conceived of prayer only as a medium for making our wants known, like calling the grocer and reading a list of items one wants delivered.

(TIM *has seated self at desk and is fingering radio stuff, yet listening to* MOTHER'S *remarks.*)

MRS. LAKE (*continuing*): I sometimes think about it when I hear you sending out your CQ signal, "I am seeking you." Many of your signals go unacknowledged, but when someone does respond, you have a nice chat. God must send out lots of CQ signals to His children. His heart yearns to chat with them about mutual interests, but His CQ goes unacknowledged. Maybe He has some important information for you right now, if you would just tune in and listen. (TIM *shakes head negatively, as if skeptical.*) Or maybe He has something more important than finding a job to talk about.

TIM: What could be more important than that right now?

MRS. LAKE: He might want to send you to help somebody, like some of those police dispatches you intercept.

TIM: For instance—.

MRS. LAKE: Remember the other day you listened to a broadcast on a lost boy? He was physically lost, but maybe there are some spiritually lost persons whom God would like to alert you to seek. You know there are many persons missing from Heaven who ought to be there. (TIM *shrugs slightly.*)

MRS. LAKE (*continuing*): Sometimes you hear them say there's a man down at such and such a place. Maybe there are other boys down with discouragement and in a worse strait than you are, because they have no place to eat or sleep while they're looking for work. Maybe God wants to tell you to go lift them up, instead of feeling sorry for yourself.

(TIM *shrugs with impatience as he puts earphones back on. He appears to be listening, then takes off earphones again.*)

TIM (*mimicking*): "Car 10, are you available? Car 10 are you available?" And car 10 is probably parked in front of some honky-tonk, and Officer O'Dooley is probably inside, playing a pinball machine.

MRS. LAKE: What was it the dispatcher said?

TIM: Are you available?

MRS. LAKE: Well *are* you? (*Pauses as if to let it soak in.*) I have a suspicion that if you were really available, and your main thought in life was to be on call for God's messages and to respond to them, you'd find this other problem would be taken care of.

TIM: Maybe you're right. I'll give it some thought. (*While he is speaking he rises and picks up his sweater and puts it on.*)

MRS. LAKE: If you'll talk to God and let Him talk to you, I'm sure you'll find things working out.

TIM (*walking toward door*): Maybe so. But prayer has always seemed like such a nebulous, intangible sort of thing to me.

MRS. LAKE (*reaching into Bible*): Let me read a little poem I keep here:

> If radio's slim fingers
>   Can pluck a melody
> From night and toss it over
>   A continent or sea;
>
> If petaled white notes
>   Of a violin
> Are blown across a mountain,
>   Or a city's din;
>
> If songs like crimson roses
>   Are culled from thin, blue air,
> Why should mortals wonder
>   If God answers prayer?[1]

TIM: You've kind of got me cornered, Mom. There's nothing left to say.

MRS. LAKE: Except that you'll talk and listen to God.

[1] Author unknown.

TIM (*patting her shoulder*): I'm going for a walk to think things out, Mom, and I just might tune in on that short-wave band to Heaven.

(*As* TIM *exits,* MRS. LAKE *drops to knees.*)

THANKSGIVING PROGRAM

A Playlet: Queer Thanksgivings[1]

CAST OF CHARACTERS

TOM TANNER, *in lounging robe, seated in an armchair with crutches leaning against it*

LAURA TANNER, *his wife, wearing a cotton print dress, seated nearby patching worn clothing*

TIMMIE TANNER, *their eight-year-old son, clad in faded jeans, seated on a footstool*

MR. *and* MRS. REED, *a well-dressed, middle-aged couple*

SETTING: Thanksgiving Eve in the bare, but neat and clean, home of the Tanners.

SCENE: *The family are about to have evening devotions. Mr. Tanner is holding a Bible. Another Bible is on the table.* MRS. TANNER *lays down her mending and picks up the Bible.*

ॐ   ॐ   ॐ

TIMMIE: Johnnie's folks have a big turkey at their house. I saw the delivery boy bring it. If Daddy hadn't had polio and been out of work, we'd have a

[1]Originally published by *Training Union Magazine,* November, 1953. Used by permission.

turkey too, wouldn't we? And then we'd have something to give thanks for.

MR. TANNER: Wait a minute, Son; you don't have to have a turkey before you can be thankful.

MRS. TANNER: Of course you don't. We can be thankful for what we *are,* not what we *have.*

TIMMIE: That's queer. Daddy would have to be thankful for being a cripple.

MRS. TANNER: You don't understand, Timmie—.

MR. TANNER (*interrupting*): I can recall some queer thanksgivings in the Bible. Remember the man named Jonah who was disobedient when God wanted him to go on a missionary journey and preach the Gospel? A big fish swallowed him, and this is what Jonah says happened. (*Has turned to Jonah 2:6-9 as he talked and now reads as follows*): "I went down to the bottoms of the mountains; the earth with her bars was about me forever; yet hast thou brought up my life from corruption, O Lord my God. When my soul fainted within me I remembered the Lord: and my prayer came in unto thee, into thine holy temple. They that observe lying vanities forsake their own mercy. But I will sacrifice unto thee with the voice of thanksgiving; I will pay that that I have vowed. Salvation is of the Lord." Now wasn't that a queer thanksgiving?

MRS. TANNER: And Timmie, you remember about Daniel's being thrown into the lions' den, don't you? Just before that happened he had been giving thanks. (*As she talks, she has opened the Bible and found Dan. 6:10.*) Here it is: "Now when Daniel knew that the writing was signed, he went into his house; and his windows being open in his chamber toward Jerusalem, he kneeled upon his knees three times a day, and prayed, and gave thanks before his God, as he did aforetime."

MR. TANNER: And when Paul and Silas were thrown into prison, they gave thanks, for we read in Acts 16:25: "And at midnight Paul and Silas prayed, and sang praises unto God: and the prisoners heard them." Singing praises would certainly be a form of thanksgiving.

MRS. TANNER: It was about the same way with Peter in prison—. (*She is interrupted by a knock. She goes to the door and finds* MR. *and* MRS. REED *there.*)

MRS. TANNER: Good evening. Won't you come in?

MRS. REED (*as they enter*): Thank you. Probably you don't remember us, but we met at the hospital.

MR. TANNER: Indeed I do. Your son had polio too. We were in the same ward after we began to convalesce.

(*While* MR. TANNER *has been talking,* MRS. TANNER *has pulled up chairs and seated the guests.*)

MRS. TANNER: Oh, yes, how *is* your son?

MRS. REED: Completely recovered and back in high school. He thinks he may even be on the basketball team.

MR. TANNER: Fine! I haven't got along that fast, but—.

Mrs. Tanner (*breaking in*): We're so thankful to God that he recovered at all.

Mr. Reed: It was the spirit of thankfulness and the joy you seemed to have inside you that impressed us.

Mrs. Reed: Maybe you didn't realize it, but we were within earshot the day the doctor told you he didn't know when you'd be able to work again. You said, "Well, Doc, I'm sure the Lord knows all about it, and His Book tells me that all things work together for good, so I'll just try to be patient until I see what the good is."

Mr. Reed: And your wife said, "The Lord will provide for our needs."

Mrs. Reed: She quoted a Scripture verse too, something about "He that spared not his own Son, but delivered him up for us all, how shall he not with him also freely give us all things?"

Mr. Reed: We puzzled over that for several days. Finally we looked up that pastor who called on you and asked him to explain to us.

Mrs. Reed: And we were saved right there in his study.

Mr. Reed: So today we're here to deliver something the Lord has provided. (*He steps out and returns wtih a basket loaded with groceries. Sticking out the top are a pair of feet belonging to a fowl. Timmie jumps up and claps his hands.*)

Mr. Tanner: How can we *ever* thank you!

Mr. Reed: Don't thank us—thank God. Excuse us

now; we've got to run along and pick up our son.

(MR. *and* MRS. REED *have both risen.* MRS. TANNER *follows them to the door.*)

MR. TANNER (*as they leave*): God bless you!

MRS. TANNER (*turning back into the room*): The Lord *does* provide. How I praise Him!

MR. TANNER (*picking up his Bible*): "In everything give thanks: for this is the will of God in Christ Jesus concerning you" (I Thess. 5:18). You see, Timmie, God's Word means just what it says. "In *everything* give thanks." If I had not had polio, Mr. and Mrs. Reed might never have found the Saviour.

TIMMIE (*who has been poking around into the contents of the basket while his father talked*): And we wouldn't have had this turkey either.

MRS. TANNER: Praise God from whom *all* blessings flow!

(*Curtain*)

CHRISTMAS PROGRAM

A Play: "Joy to the World"[1]

CAST OF CHARACTERS

MRS. *and* MRS. KINCAID, *middle-aged tourists from Chicago*

LARRY SCOTT, *garage proprietor and youth director at his church.*

REV. THEODORE BROWN, *pastor*

CHILDREN, *participants in Christmas program*

PROPERTIES NEEDED

A Gideon Bible, or one similar to it

Several pieces of luggage

Winter coats and hats

A handkerchief

A large dinner bell

A large, gaily decorated Christmas tree

PRODUCTION NOTES

If need be, the sound of the church bell's ringing in Scene 1 may be made with a large dinner bell.

Be sure that Mr. and Mrs. Kincaid speak distinctly enough for their last lines in Scene 2 to be understood.

[1] Originally published in the *Training Union Magazine*, December, 1953. Used by permission.

Scene 1

SETTING: *A shabby hotel room. An unopened Gideon Bible rests on the dresser. The* KINCAIDS *have obviously been quarreling.* MRS. KINCAID *is crumpled up in a chair, dabbing her eyes with a handkerchief.* MR. KINCAID *is walking the floor in an irritated manner.*

        ❧   ❧   ❧

MR. KINCAID: Can you think of anything worse! Stranded in this dump on Christmas Eve—not a bar or a night club or even a measly movie. Not a train or a bus in or out! Not even a TV in the lobby! Why couldn't the car have broken down in a *city!*

MRS. KINCAID: If you'd only stop your ranting! It's all your fault anyway. If you hadn't got that crazy idea of spending Christmas on the old farm we'd have been having a real celebration with the bunch back in Chicago where we belong.

As for your bars and night clubs, you didn't expect to find them on a farm in the middle of nowhere anyway, did you? And why moan about the trains? You wouldn't take a train when you could. No, sir, you were too good for dirty old trains! You preferred your own comfortable car. I told you how it'd be!

And if you must have entertainment, why don't you go to that church program the kid at the garage invited you to? Or, if you want to read, there's a

Book on the dresser. Ought to be something exciting in that!

(*Church bell rings.*)

MR. KINCAID: Oh, shut up! Listen, what's that? Sounds like a bell ringing.

MRS. KINCAID: Curfew, I expect. It's seven o'clock. You have the whole evening before you to enjoy this wonderful bridal suite. I bet that bed hasn't more than a hundred lumps in the mattress. Just imagine it's one of those pine-bough beds you sleep on when you go camping, or the straw mattress you had when you were a kid!

MR. KINCAID: Oh, what's the use of being sarcastic? (*Pauses.*) I wish I *were* a boy on Christmas Eve again. I suppose I *would* be going to the church program. My folks were God-fearing people. Old Deacon Hobbs would be standing up to read. He was so nearsighted he always held his Bible right up to his nose like this. (*Picks up Bible to illustrate and continues leafing through it as he reminisces.*) Then we'd have a tree lit and the treats distributed. What an agony it was, waiting for your name to be called. (*Sits down in a chair and continues leafing through the Bible.*)

MRS. KINCAID: We had a tree at the church too. I remember I always wanted the tinsel angel on the top branch.

MR. KINCAID: You would!

MRS. KINCAID (*ignoring thrust*): And we sang songs. (*Hums a snatch of a Christmas carol.*)

MR. KINCAID: Why, here's the very words the deacon always read. I can hear his voice now: "For unto you is born this day in the city of David a Saviour which is Christ the Lord. And this shall be a sign unto you; Ye shall find the babe wrapped in swaddling clothes, lying in a manger. And suddenly there was with the angel a multitude of the heavenly host praising God, and saying, Glory to God in the highest, and on earth peace good will toward men."

MRS. KINCAID: Peace! Who is there nowadays that knows the meaning of the word? Joy! All the world is searching for it, but has anyone found it?

MR. KINCAID: You know, mad as I was, I couldn't help but notice that garage man. *He* seemed to have it. You remember he said *he* was going to the church program when his little kid asked us if we were going. I believe that man had peace—.

MRS. KINCAID: I guess the youngster had joy, the way he was jitterbugging around. Wonder what he'll get on the Christmas tree. I bet his eyes would pop out at that train we've got for your sister Ollie's kid—.

MR. KINCAID: Oh, I'd forgotten about all that junk in the car! That crate of oranges will freeze.

MRS. KINCAID: There's all that candy and nuts too.

MR. KINCAID (*hesitantly, in an embarrassed manner*): Madge, what do you say, why not make the best of things? Would you be willing to get that stuff out of the car and go over to the Christmas tree at the church?

MRS. KINCAID (*starting to put on wraps*): I believe I'd like it. We'll wrap up the train and put it on the tree for the little boy.

MR. KINCAID (*pulling on his overcoat*): And the oranges and candy will be a treat for all the rest of them.

(*They go out, humming a Christmas carol.*)

SCENE 2

SETTING: *The front of a church auditorium with a Christmas tree and holiday decorations. Pianist softly plays "It Came upon the Midnight Clear." Congregation is assembled and pastor rises and addresses them.*

PASTOR BROWN: We welcome all of you to this celebration of our Lord's birthday. Our young people have charge of our program tonight. I'm going to ask the director, Larry Scott, to come forward and preside.

(MR. SCOTT *has been seated near the front. He stands up as* MR. *and* MRS. KINCAID *are ushered to a pew across the aisle from him.*)

MR. SCOTT: I'm sure there's a great deal of joy in the hearts of all of us as we gather here tonight. My heart has been singing all day because this season so constantly reminds me of how much I have in which to rejoice in the coming of Christ to earth.

It is in such a spirit that I welcome all of you here. We're especially glad to see in our group Mr. and Mrs. Kincaid, of Chicago, whose car broke down and left them stranded here. Let's all give them so warm a welcome they'll forget their disappointment.

(MR. SCOTT *announced the program. Have two or three Christmas numbers, such as music and readings.*)

MR. SCOTT: It wouldn't be Christmas without the story of the nativity. Our pastor is going to tell us in his own words about the first Christmas. Pastor Brown:

(PASTOR BROWN *tells the Christmas story, bringing out the fact that Christ was born to die for man's sins. He closes as follows*):

PASTOR BROWN: If we too will follow the star, if we will accept Christ as our own personal Saviour, and then make Him the Lord of our lives, yielding them to Him, using them in His service, we too will find peace and joy. Let's all sing "Joy to the World!"

MRS. KINCAID (*turning to husband as they rise, and placing her hand on his arm*): That's the way we can have peace, by trusting Christ as our Saviour—.

MR. KINCAID (*clasping her hand in his*): And we'll have joy as we begin life anew, serving our Lord.

(*All sing "Joy to the World!"*)

NO MORE X-MAS[1]

CAST OF CHARACTERS

JEAN BLAKESLY, *Primary-age girl*
KENT BLAKESLY, *Junior-age boy*
RUTH BLAKESLY, *teen-age girl*
MARCIA BLAKESLY, *their mother*
ART BLAKESLY, *their father*
GRANDMA BLAKESLY, *his mother*

SETTING: *The action takes place in an average family dining-living room. There are two entrances, one supposedly from the outside with a window near it. Furnishings should include a dining table, a telephone, and a large mirror. There should be a couple of carelessly placed Christmas decorations.*

TIME: *Two successive evenings the week before Christmas*

🍀   🍀   🍀

SCENE I

JEAN *is standing behind the table, facing audience, and is engaged in coloring a Christmas card she has made. Her grandmother is seated to the side front,*

[1]Originally published in the *Training Union Magazine*, December, 1955. Used by permission.

knitting. In a chair there is a dainty apron which MARCIA BLAKESLY *will work on for a Christmas gift.* KENT *enters.*

KENT: Whatcha doin'?

JEAN: Making a Christmas card to send to my Sunday school teacher.

KENT: Bet she won't even look at it. (*He picks up a newspaper and turns to the comic section.*)

JEAN: How do you spell "Merry Christmas"?

KENT (*handing her a section of the paper and pointing*): You can copy it off there.

JEAN (*after copying for a moment*): Oh! I'm not going to have room for it all. The "merry" took up too much space.

KENT: Cross it out and start a new line. Print smaller.

JEAN: That wouldn't look nice to have a crossed-out line. Oh, what can I do?

KENT: Write Christmas the short way: "X-mas." (*Makes a crisscross in air to illustrate.*)

JEAN: Oh, good! That'll work. I can get "X-mas" in the space.

(GRANDMA BLAKESLY *looks distressed, but before she can speak,* ART BLAKESLY *enters, followed by his wife. He is wearing an overcoat and carrying his hat.*)

GRANDMA BLAKESLY: Why, Art, is it time for prayer meeting already?

ART: I have to go back to the store, Mother. You know we're staying open evenings now on account of the holiday trade. We have to get the business while we can. People are in a buying mood, and we have to cash in on it. Maybe Marcia or one of the children will go with you tonight.

(*His mother shakes her head sadly. His wife follows him to the door, telling him good-by. She then picks up her sewing, sits down, and begins to work on it. As she does so, she addresses the children.*)

MARCIA: Better put your things away now, Jean. It's time you were thinking about getting to bed. Kent, have you finished your lessons?

KENT: Yes'm.

(RUTH *enters, carrying coat and scarf, dressed for a party.*)

JEAN: You look pretty, Ruth. Are you going with Grandma to prayer meeting?

RUTH (*laughing as she checks herself in the mirror*): In these clothes? I should say not! I'm going to a party at school.

JEAN: But I heard your youth director say your group was going to sing Christmas carols for the shut-ins after prayer meeting. She said that would show you really had Christmas in your heart.

RUTH: So what, Smarty? I can't be two places at the same time, and this Christmas party comes just once a year. (*She slips on her coat and goes to the door.*) 'By, everybody.

MARCIA (*who has never paused in her sewing*): Good-by. Now, Jean, it's your bedtime. Skip along.

JEAN: But, Mother, you haven't heard my prayers.

MARCIA: I know, but I can't stop just now. Kent, you'd better go to bed, too.

KENT: This early? Aw, Mom, I'm not a kid any more. And I wanted you to drill me on my part for the program. It's a play about people who forgot why we have Christmas.

MARCIA: You heard me, Kent. I just do not have time tonight.

KENT: Aw, Mom.

GRANDMA: I can look after the children before I go to prayer meeting, Marcia. Go ahead, children. I'll be up in a few minutes.

JEAN: Will you tell us a story, too?

KENT: Sure she will. I bet I'm ready first.

(KENT *darts out of the room and* JEAN *dashes after him.* GRANDMA *puts away her knitting and prepares to follow. The phone rings.* MARCIA *sighs as she lays her sewing down and answers it.*)

MARCIA (*on telephone*): Hello. (*Pause*) Oh, Grace, not tomorrow. I'd forgotten all about those cookies for the Children's Home. I don't see how I can possibly bake any. I just haven't time. I'm going to be working until the wee small hours now, trying to finish our gift for Art's sister.

(*As* MARCIA *listens,* GRANDMA *lays her knitting aside and quietly exits.*)

MARCIA: Yes, I know, but I wish they'd choose some other time of year for things like baking cookies for orphans. (*Pause.*) His little ones . . . in his name . . . our birthday gift to Christ? Well, if you put it that way, I can't very well refuse. Put me down for three dozen. Maybe Mother Blakesly will feel like baking them. Good-by. (*She replaces the phone and stands as if thinking, then speaks aloud.*)

MARCIA: She'll probably want chocolate chips for the cookies. I'd better check right now and see whether there are any. (*She exits as the curtain closes.*)

SCENE 2

Later the same evening. Only a table lamp is burning. GRANDMA returns from prayer meeting, takes off her hat and coat, and sits down to read her Bible. Lamplight should spot her head and hands. Carolers begin singing off stage. GRANDMA lifts her head as if listening, then goes to the window and looks out.

GRANDMA: How sweet that was! I know poor old bedridden Mr. Martin enjoyed it, and so did I. God bless those young carolers. I wish Ruth—. (*She picks up her Bible again and reads Luke 2:7 aloud.*) "And she brought forth her firstborn son, and wrapped him in swaddling clothes, and laid him in a manger; because there was no room for them in the inn."

No room for Him in the inn at Bethlehem. And no room for Him in many American hearts and homes either. They've crossed Christ out of Christmas. They've substituted an *X*—symbol of an unknown quantity. *X* marks the spot where Christ should be, but isn't allowed. Not room enough for Him on a

Christmas card. Not room enough for Him in their lives. No time for deeds of mercy in His name. Parties and gifts for one another, but none for Him whose anniversary Christmas is! (*She bows her head as the curtain closes.*)

Scene 3

Two evenings before Christmas. Family are gathered around the table where a meal has evidently just been finished. Everyone seems tired and cross.

JEAN: Tomorrow night is Christmas Eve.

KENT: You don't have to go to the store tomorrow night, do you, Daddy?

ART: Sure don't, Son. The store closes at 5:00 P.M.

RUTH: And school closed today. Don't anyone disturb me until noon tomorrow. I'm catching up on my sleep.

MARCIA (*peevishly*): Not yet, my darling daughter. Don't forget we have a houseful of company coming to Christmas dinner, and some of them are your guests. You'll have to help get ready for them.

(RUTH *looks pouty.*)

ART (*disgruntled*): You mean I'll have to dress up and won't get to relax on Christmas Day? Who's coming?

MARCIA (*with spirit*): As if I hadn't told you! *Your* sister and her family of *seven*, to mention just a few of them.

KENT: Will I have to be dressed up, too? Can't I

go out and ride my new bike—that is, if I get one?

JEAN: And I'll want to skate—if I get my new skates.

GRANDMA (*shaking her head and addressing her son*): Art, I wonder where your father and I failed in rearing you. . . . (*She pauses as if choked up and about to cry. All eyes turn her way.*)

ART: Why, Mother, what's the matter?

MARCIA: Has anybody said anything to hurt your feelings?

GRANDMA: It's the Lord Jesus Christ whose feelings must be hurt. Christmas is the anniversary of His leaving His home in Heaven and coming to earth so that there might be love, joy, and peace among His people, but what does He see? He sees Himself crowded out of Christmas. He hears grumbling and bickering. No one gives *Him* a thought. Business, pleasure, presents, rush, rush, rush! No time or place for Christ!

ART (*thoughtfully*): I reckon you're right, Mother. I hadn't thought about it in that way. Guess I've been substituting a dollar sign for the Christ in Christmas.

JEAN (*not comprehending*): Oh, Daddy, did you? I used an X instead, but I didn't know you could use a dollar sign, too!

KENT: Silly! You don't understand what you are talking about.

JEAN: I know what Grandma prayed with us last night. She said, "Dear God, please help this family to see that they can't cross Christ out of Christmas and have anything lovely left." Didn't you, Grandma? (GRANDMA *appears embarrassed.*)

MARCIA: Grandma is right. Each of us, in one way or another, has crossed Christ out of Christmas. That's why we're tired and cranky, and fussing about Christmas Day instead of looking forward to it with joy.

RUTH: I'll be happy if I get a new watch. (*She glances at her father.*) I really need one, too.

KENT: Say, we're just like those people in the play. We've forgotten why we have Christmas.

ART: That's right, Son, and I think it would help us to read the Christmas story again. Then we'll ask God to help us not to substitute an X—or a dollar sign either—for "Christ" in "Christmas."

JEAN: And we'll have a lovely Christmas yet!

(*The curtain falls as* KENT *hands a Bible to his father.*)

DEAR OLD EBENEZER [1]

CAST OF CHARACTERS

MRS. JORDAN
GEORGE JORDAN, *her husband*
WILLIE JORDAN, *their Junior son*
BETTY JORDAN, *their daughter, also of Junior age*
MRS. BANKS, *of the P.T.A.*
MRS. WATERS, *of the Thimble Club*
RADIO REPAIR MAN
CENSUS TAKER
REV. WM. LAKE, *Baptist pastor*

SETTING: *All four scenes are laid in the living room of the Jordans, who have recently moved into the community.*

ঙ্গ   ঙ্গ   ঙ্গ

SCENE 1

The living room is disordered. Mrs. Jordan is unpacking a trunk. She takes out an envelope tied with a colored cord, holds it up, and then looks around thoughtfully. She speaks to herself.

MRS. JORDAN: Let's see; where shall I put this? I wouldn't want to lose it for anything on earth. Dear

[1]Originally published in the *Training Union Magazine,* May, 1951. Used by permission.

Ebenezer, how many fond memories I have of you. I know; I'll put it in my Bible for the present.

(*She places it in the Bible on the library table. Her husband enters, picking his way around chairs and over piles of things.*)

MR. JORDAN: Where's the saw and the hammer? I want to fix up a work bench in the basement.

MRS. JORDAN: Go 'long with you—that workshop can wait. I need some more shelves in the pantry. You get at them. And as soon as the ground dries out a little I want you to spade up the back yard. I got the grandest garden assortment from the breakfast-food top I sent in. It was even better than it sounded over the radio. There's an iris root and a peony. We'll have blossoms for next spring from some of the plants, besides all the aster blooms next fall. I had to send only a dollar with the top too. I do want a nice flower garden.

MR. JORDAN: Well, I guess you can have one. There's a nice yard.

MRS. JORDAN: Yes, I told the real estate agent, "I want a place with a good yard where we'll be close to both grade and high schools, because while the children aren't ready for high school yet, it won't be many years until they are." Here, you carry this trunk to the basement and I'll see about dinner.

(*As they exit, MR. JORDAN carrying the trunk on his shoulder, BETTY and WILLIE enter and mess around with things in the room.*)

BETTY: Oh, lookee, here's Mother's Bible. Isn't it big? Let's find about Daniel and the lions.

WILLIE: No, I'd rather hear about David and the giant.

(*They start to wrestle over the Book, and the letter falls out.*)

BETTY: Oh, wait; it's a letter. Let's see—.

WILLIE: 'Tain't yours. You'd better leave it alone.

BETTY: Maybe it's our report cards from the Salem school—.

(*Mother enters.*)

MRS. JORDAN: Here, watch out! Look what you're doing. Give that to me.

BETTY: What is it, Mother?

WILLIE: Let us see what's inside.

MRS. JORDAN: Never you mind; it doesn't concern you. It's very valuable, and don't you ever let me catch you laying hands on it again. Now, scat! Go wash your hands. Dinner's ready.

(*The children exit hastily.* MRS. JORDAN *wipes the letter on her apron.*)

MRS. JORDAN: Let's see. I'd better put this out of their reach. I wouldn't lose it for anything. Dear old Ebenezer! I know, I'll put it here under the piano scarf.

SCENE 2

The time is a week later. The living room is neat and orderly. MRS. JORDAN *is seated, stitching on some white material. A knock sounds, but she does not hear it. It is repeated. She opens door.*

MRS. JORDAN: Oh, how do you do? Come in. Did you knock more than once? Will you sit down? It's so hard to hear on this street. I told Mr. Jordan last night we ought to have a bell. He said he'd get me one for our wedding anniversary, the chime kind that rings differently for the front and back doors. Of course, our anniversary isn't until next fall, but it will be nice to look forward to.

MRS. BANKS: I'm Mrs. Banks, Mrs. Jordan. I'm Betty's room mother. I called to see if you wouldn't like to join the P.T.A. We want 100 per cent membership, and we need you. Won't you come to the meeting Friday at the school?

MRS. JORDAN: Thank you, I'd like to. I always belonged to the P.T.A. back in Salem where we moved from. In fact, I was one of the officers.

MRS. BANKS: Oh, fine! I venture to predict they'll make an officer of you next year. Good material is always in demand.

MRS. JORDAN: I'll be glad to do anything I can.

MRS. BANKS (*rising to go*): I'll look for you Friday then.

MRS. JORDAN: Thank you, I'll be there. Come back again.

(MRS. BANKS *exits.* MRS. JORDAN *resumes her sewing. Another knock sounds. She admits a man.*)

MAN: I'm the repair man from the Radio Shop. You phoned for us?

MRS. JORDAN: Oh, yes, my husband wants you to put up an outside aerial for him. He's quite a radio fan and likes to tune in on foreign broadcasts. Come this way and I'll show you where he wants it.

(*As they move off the scene she is heard speaking.*)

MRS. JORDAN: He said to tell you to make it real substantial. We don't want to have to be having it done all over again next year.

(*She is summoned back almost immediately by another knock. A lady is at the door.*)

MRS. WATERS: How do you do? Are you Mrs. Jordan? I'm your neighbor across the street. My name is Waters.

MRS. JORDAN: How do you do, Mrs. Waters? How nice of you to call. Do have a chair. I was just fixing a little curtain for the attic window. Of course, the attic isn't finished and we don't use it, but I thought it would look more homey from the outside if I had a curtain up there.

MRS. WATERS: Of course. You bought this place, didn't you?

MRS. JORDAN: No, we haven't yet, but we're thinking about it.

MRS. WATERS: You couldn't find a better neighborhood. I know you will like everyone; they almost all own their places. By the way, we have a neighborhood Thimble Club. I thought you might like to join. We meet every third Wednesday in one of the homes. Just now we're sewing for the refugees. We take turns about entertaining in the order our names come in the alphabet, only we started at Z and are going backward. It meets with me next time.

MRS. JORDAN: Thank you so much. Let's see. I'm J. I guess I'll be straightened up by the time my turn comes.

MRS. WATERS: Oh, my, yes. There are a number of members. It might be a year before it got to you.

MRS. JORDAN: Fine! Why, yes, I think I'd like to join. Will you excuse me a moment? There is a man here to fix the radio aerial. I'll be right back.

MRS. WATERS: I have to go anyway, Mrs. Jordan, and I'll be looking for you next Wednesday. We meet at ten, and bring a covered dish.

(*She exits by front door. MRS. JORDAN goes out the back. The children come in front door. BETTY starts to play the piano noisily. WILLIE comes over and reaches for a novelty on top of the piano. He skews the scarf around, and the letter falls to the floor.*)

WILLIE: Oh, here's that letter again.

BETTY: You know what Mother said, You better leave it alone. Oh, Mother! Come see what Willie's got.

(MRS. JORDAN *enters; cuffs* WILLIE. *Children scamper off. She wipes off letter on apron.*)

MRS. JORDAN: Dear Ebenezer! Let's see, where can I put this so the children won't get it? I wouldn't lose it for anything. I know: I'll clip it to the back of this calendar.

SCENE 3

A month has passed. MRS. JORDAN *is again in the living room, darning socks, when a knock is heard. A man stands at the door.*

MAN: How do you do? I'm from the First Baptist Church down the street. We're checking up on the religious census of the community. Will you give me the information on your family? You're new in the neighborhood, aren't you?

MRS. JORDAN: Come in and sit down. I'm a Baptist too. I've done the very thing you're doing. We took a census back in Salem not more than a month before we left there. Just let me have your cards and I'll fill them out.

(CENSUS TAKER *talks while she writes.*)

MAN: We have Sunday school every Sunday morning at 9:30 and Young People's in the evening at 6:30. We have classes for every member of the family and we hope you will all start coming right away. I guess you know that every Baptist church is always in need of workers. We hope you'll come and feel so much at home that you'll want to go right to work. Could we come by for you tomorrow?

MRS. JORDAN: Thank you; that won't be necessary. I will try to at least get the children over. You know how much work it is getting settled in a new place. We ought to get started right away.

MAN: We'd be happy to have you put your membership in with us.

MRS. JORDAN: Well, I don't know. I've been thinking about it, but I don't know how long we'll be here. But thank you anyway.

(CENSUS TAKER *exits.*)

SCENE 4

BETTY *and* WILLIE *come in wearing spring clothes and carrying Bibles.*)

WILLIE: Hey, Mom, where are you? Mother, the preacher said he was coming to see you. He was awful sorry you aren't feeling well.

BETTY: Mrs. Black said—Mother, are you listening? —Mrs. Black said to tell you they're counting on your being at the missionary meeting Thursday.

MRS. JORDAN (*from off stage*): All right.

(*Children look at funny papers.* BETTY *opens her Bible and takes out card.*)

BETTY: Look at the swell picture I got for being 100 per cent all last month. I'm going to hang it up. Where can I put it? (*Looks around. Spies calendar.*) We don't need this old calendar.

(*Grabs calendar off wall and throws it on chair. Puts picture in its place. Stands off and admires it.* WILLIE *spies letter on calendar.*)

WILLIE: Oh, Betty, look what you did. Mother, Betty threw that letter away.

(MRS. JORDAN *enters; runs and picks up letter, giving* BETTY *a shove as she does so.*)

MRS. JORDAN: Oh, my precious letter! I don't know what on earth I'd do if I lost it. Now, scat! Both of you!

(*Children exit hastily. She wipes letter on apron.*)

MRS. JORDAN: Dear Ebenezer. I know; I'll put it in this vase.

(*She puts it in vase on piano. A knock is heard. The preacher is at the door.*)

MRS. JORDAN: Oh, come in, Pastor Lake.

PASTOR LAKE: Excuse me for stopping now, but I'm due at another engagement. I heard you weren't well and I wanted to let you know we missed you. You know, we've been hoping you would put your membership in with us.

MRS. JORDAN: It was kind of you to come. I haven't been real sick. I don't think I should put my letter in until I'm better acquainted with the people. After all, we don't know how long we'll be here—.

PASTOR LAKE: But, Mrs. Jordan, you know we're a missionary Baptist church, you know what we stand for, what we preach. Can't you come in and unite with us in our efforts to win the lost souls? We'll be glad to take you under the watchcare of the church and send for your letter—.

MRS. JORDAN (*interrupting*): Oh, I have my letter, Pastor Lake, and it's addressed to the First Baptist Church, but as I say, I don't know how long we'll be here.

(PASTOR *rises to depart, and she follows him to the door. Meanwhile, the children have come back in and are monkeying around the piano.* WILLIE *again skews the scarf around, and the vase crashes to the floor just as* MRS. JORDAN *returns to the room.*

The children make a hasty exit. MRS. JORDAN *picks up the letter and wipes it on her apron.*)

MRS. JORDAN: Dear old Ebenezer Church back in Salem.

(*She looks around for a place to put letter, then speaks to her husband, who has just entered.*)

MRS. JORDAN: I don't know where to keep my church letter. I wouldn't lose it for anything.

MR. JORDAN: What difference would it make?

MRS. JORDAN (*in shocked tone*): What *difference* would it make?

MR. JORDAN: That's what I said. You plan for next season's garden. You plan for years ahead when the kids will be in high school. You join everything else in the community. But when they invite you to join the church, you say we don't know how long we'll be here and that you don't know the people well enough. And then you take on about your church letter. If you ask me, all that letter stands for is sentimental poppycock. If it were a symbol of true Christianity, you'd have turned it over to the church here weeks ago—.

MRS. JORDAN (*interrupting*): Don't you dare talk to me like that, George Jordan! And yet . . . I guess a lot of what you say is right . . . I hadn't realized until you put it that way. Here, I'll put it in your desk until next Sunday. Then I'll go down at the morning service and give it to Brother Lake.

MR. JORDAN: And I'll apply for baptism. Ever since the first time I heard Pastor Lake preach I've known I should, but I've been waiting for you. I thought I'd go in whenever you did.

MRS. JORDAN: Oh, George!

(*Curtain*)

ALL THERE IS OF US[1]

You can use this play on the stewardship of life in October or at any time during the year.

CAST OF CHARACTERS

BOB, *a young serviceman home on furlough*
NANCY, *his girl friend*
MR. *and* MRS. GLASGOW, *her parents*
KYLE SMITH, *their pastor*
JACK PORTER, *youth director*
DEACON JOHNSON
PANEL MEMBERS:
    JOHN WHEAT, *member of Congress*
    GEORGE FRENCH, *attorney and broker*
    DEAN JORDAN, *artist*
    BETTY BAKER, *wheel-chair Christian*

PRODUCTION NOTES

DR. SMITH and JORDAN should be about forty years of age; JOHNSON, GLASGOW, WHEAT, and FRENCH, older.

NANCY might wear a corsage.

For the music in scene 3, use classical or semiclassical records.

[1]Originally published in the *Training Union Magazine,* September, 1953. Used by permission.

If a wheel chair is not available, let BETTY use crutches.

SCENE 1

SETTING: *The living room of an average American home. NANCY and BOB are seated on the davenport engaged in low-toned, laughing conversation when MR. and MRS. GLASGOW enter, dressed for the street.*

꙳ ꙳ ꙳

BOB (*stands*): Oh, are you going out? Let me tell you again what a wonderful dinner that was, Mrs. Glasgow. That was part of my furlough dream come true. You know, good, home-cooked American food is one of the chief things a GI looks forward to.

MRS. GLASGOW: Thank you, Bob. It pleases me to know you enjoyed it. You must drop in often while you are home.

BOB (*looking at NANCY*): I guess I will.

NANCY (*to her parents*): Let's see, this is Friday night. I've forgotten where it is you go—?

MR. GLASGOW: It's Stewardship Night at the church. The Young People's group is sponsoring it.

NANCY: Of course! I read about it in the bulletin Sunday.

MRS. GLASGOW: I wish you two would go with us.

NANCY: Bob has so little time—.

BOB (*interrupts*): What is it you're going to?

MR. GLASGOW: Stewardship Night. There's going

to be a panel discussion which will be right worth while.

MRS. GLASGOW: Tell Bob who the panel members are.

MR. GLASGOW (*marking off the names on his fingers*): There's Dean Jordan—.

NANCY (*interrupting*): Isn't he the artist who did the murals in the new post office?

MR. GLASGOW (*nodding assent*): And Representative Wheat—George French—.

BOB: You mean French, the big investment broker and attorney?

MR. GLASGOW: That's right—and Betty Baker—.

NANCY (*surprised*): Betty Baker? (*Turns to* BOB.) Bob, do you remember Betty? (BOB *nods*.) She was injured in a car crash last year. She's paralyzed from her waist down.

MR. GLASGOW: That's the setup. Dr. Smith will act as moderator of the discussion. It's going to be interesting. You'd better come.

(BOB *and* NANCY *look at each other questioningly*.)

NANCY: Whatever Bob says—.

BOB (*hesitantly*): Well, I'll tell you. I was counting on taking Nancy down to Barrymore's later. If this panel business won't last too late and you won't care if I take Nancy there afterward—.

MRS. GLASGOW: You can do both. We'll see you at church.

(*Curtain*)

SCENE 2

SETTING: *The front of a church auditorium.* PANEL
MEMBERS *are seated at a table on the platform.*
PASTOR *sits at one end; girl in a wheel chair, at the
other end. Three men are arranged along the side
facing audience.* MR. *and* MRS. GLASGOW *enter
from rear of auditorium and sit down in the front
pew. Then* NANCY *and* BOB *enter and sit down.*
PASTOR *rises.*

PASTOR: Good evening, friends. As you all know,
this observance of Stewardship Night is sponsored
by our Young People's group. Through the capable
efforts of our director, Jack Porter, we are to have a
panel discussion on the subject "What Is Stewardship?" At this time Mr. Porter will introduce the
participants.

MR. PORTER: I'm certainly indebted to these fine
panel members for making themselves available to
us tonight. Beginning on our pastor's left, I'll introduce them around the table. As I call their names,
each can take a bow without rising. First, the skillful
artist whose wonderful murals you have all seen in
the new post office: Dean Jordan.

(JORDAN *smiles and nods his head, as do the other
panel members as they are introduced.*)

Next, one of the successful attorneys and business-
men of our community, of the firm of French and
French, investment brokers: Mr. George French.
Third, our esteemed congressman from this district:

Representative John Wheat. And last, the gamest girl I know, beloved by all our membership: Miss Betty Baker. (MR. PORTER *bows and returns to his seat.*)

PASTOR: Before we begin our panel discussion, let's sing one stanza of "Give of Your Best to the Master." At the close, Deacon Johnson, will you lead us in prayer, asking that God will give these panel members what they are to say, and pray that we'll be willing to apply what they say to our life situations?

(ALL *sing first stanza of "Give of Your Best to the Master."*)

(MR. JOHNSON *leads in prayer.*)

PASTOR: Representative Wheat, suppose you open our discussion tonight by telling us your conception of stewardship.

WHEAT (*rising*): Dr. Smith, ladies and gentlemen: A steward, according to the dictionary, is one who superintends the affairs of another. From such a definition it is evident that he is not the owner. In a special sense, the word *steward* is used to designate an officer on board a ship who has charge of the provisions, such as food and beverages. (*Sits down.*)

PASTOR: When I rode a plane the other day, the food was in charge of a stewardess.

WHEAT (*without rising*): And she didn't own the food—she was handling it for the airline company which operated the plane. She was responsible to that company.

PASTOR: Thank you, Representative Wheat. Now, Mr. French, would you like to add anything to this definition of a steward?

FRENCH: Only this: I might point out that we have another term in the business world which conveys somewhat the same idea. It is trustee. And that word, of course, defines itself. A trustee, supposedly, is one who can be trusted. If he proves otherwise, we have another name for him: an embezzler!

PASTOR: Thank you, Mr. French. Mr. Jordan, have you anything to contribute?

JORDAN: I think we should place a little more emphasis on this point: that the trustee or steward is not only entrusted with something to manage for another, but he is supposed to handle it in a way that will be profitable to the owner. Mr. French won't mind my saying, I'm sure, that he wouldn't retain his customers long if he didn't handle their accounts in such a way as to earn dividends for them.

PASTOR: Thank you, Mr. Jordan. Any word from you, Miss Baker?

(*She shakes her head in negative.*)

PASTOR: Now that we have an understanding of the word *steward* and, hence, of *stewardship*, in the general sense of the word, let's approach the Biblical significance of the term. Representative Wheat, do you understand the term steward in the Bible to apply only to one who has been entrusted with material items such as money?

WHEAT: To infer *that* would, in my opinion, limit

the term in a degree not meant by the Author. One can be a steward of intangible as well as tangible items, and he is just as responsible for their wise handling.

PASTOR: Can you illustrate what you mean?

(*As* WHEAT *hesitates,* FRENCH *speaks up.*)

FRENCH: Brother Chairman, I think I can, if I may be permitted to speak. (PASTOR *turns to him, giving assent.*) In legal procedure, a guardian is sometimes appointed for a minor. He may not have a red cent to his own name, no real property is involved, but the guardian is no less a trustee. He is responsible for the welfare of the child, an intangible item, but one for which he is as answerable to the court as if it were a million dollars entrusted to him.

PASTOR: Thank you, Mr. French. Representative Wheat, you look as if you had something to add.

WHEAT: I can offer a personal illustration of stewardship of an intangible item. As a congressman, I have a voice or vote in the affairs of government. If I don't use my power in Congress to bring relief to oppressed or minority groups, to suppress vice, and so on, I have been a poor steward, and the people who have appointed me to represent them may take my stewardship away from me and replace me with one who, they believe, will prove more diligent and faithful.

PASTOR: Is your stewardship of office from the voters only, Representative Wheat?

WHEAT: No, it isn't. As I see it personally, I feel

that the Lord put me in office to bear influence for him. I'm *His* steward, and He may see fit to remove me from office by sickness or death if I don't prove faithful.

PASTOR: I'd like to bring out just here that, from the information I have, Representative Wheat is a faithful steward. If you will examine the record, you will find that often, as he has spoken on the floor of Congress, he has made some reference to man's responsibility to God. The fact that he is participating in this panel tonight proves that he seeks to be a good steward of his influence. (*Turns to* JORDAN.) Now, Mr. Jordan, may we ask you a question? We feel that God has endowed you with a great talent. Do *you* share Representative Wheat's idea of stewardship in respect to your talent?

JORDAN: Yes, Brother Chairman, I do. First of all, I'm responsible for the *manner* in which I use my talent. As suggested by the song we sang, I must give my best. As long as God has given me skill to paint first-rate pictures, I've no right to paint second-rate ones. To splash and daub when I'm capable of doing better would be poor stewardship.

In the second place, I'm responsible for the *purpose* for which I use my talent. I know artists who draw lewd pictures. If I were to do that, I would be an unfaithful steward of the talent my Lord has entrusted to me. In that event, I might in all justice, as Representative Wheat suggested, lose the use of my arm, or my talent might just deteriorate, as has been the case with some artists whom I know.

You know, the man in the Bible had his talent taken from him. Of course, I know that the word translated "talent" there actually refers to money. But it always gives me something to think about when I read that passage.

PASTOR: Thanks, Mr. Jordan. I might say, in case any of you are not aware of it, that a token of Mr. Jordan's sense of stewardship of talent is the posters he makes for us from time to time. The one on Stewardship Night in the lobby right now is his work. (*Turns to* BETTY BAKER.) Miss Baker, what has been in your mind during this discussion?

BETTY: A lot of things, and some of them painful. But if it will help anyone to become a faithful steward, I'm willing to talk about them.

When Mr. Jordan was talking about losing the use of his arm as a penalty for poor stewardship—.

(JORDAN *interrupts with obvious embarrassment.*)

JORDAN: Oh, I say, Miss Baker, I never thought— I didn't mean—I apologize—.

BETTY: You needn't. What you said was right, and God might be forced to deal with us in that way. And don't think I didn't wonder about it when I lost the use of my legs. I would lie for hours, my thoughts going in circles like this: Did I lose their use because I went to the wrong places on them or used them for the wrong things? Or was it because

I didn't go to the right places? In other words, was I a poor steward of them?

I prayed lots about it and finally God gave me an answer. He said, "Betty, this happened so that you could be a better steward of your time—so that you could use the time allotted to you to better advantage."

You know, time is the stuff life is made of, and if we waste it or fail to use it to serve God's purpose, we are just as much embezzlers as if we had misappropriated money. We're all going to have to answer to God for our stewardship of time.

PASTOR: Betty, would you mind telling us how you use *your* time?

BETTS (*hesitantly*): Well, I write notes and try to cheer up people who are sick or in trouble. Sometimes they're to folks here that I know personally, and sometimes they're to folks I read about, however the Lord leads.

PASTOR: I'd like for you to tell how else you use your time for God, Betty.

BETTY: Well, prayer takes a lot of my time. Some of you have seen that map of the world on my wall with all the little crosses on it. They represent missionaries. Each day I pray for a different mission field and the workers and their needs.

PASTOR: What else do you pray about, Betty?

BETTY: The Bible says to pray for those who have the rule over us; in other words, our officials. One day I pray by name for our city officials, another for the county, the state, and so on.

PASTOR: Betty, tell us, could a person be a poor steward of prayer in any way besides failing to pray?

BETTY (*silent, as if thinking*): Maybe that was what James indicated when he said, "Ye ask amiss, that ye may consume it upon your lusts," or your "selfish cravings" as another translation has it. I used to pray that I might be able to walk again. Then I realized that back of my prayer was the desire to go places and do the things that other girls my age were doing. That was poor stewardship of prayer. Now I just remind myself that "His grace is sufficient" and I pray, "Thy will be done."

PASTOR: Thank you, Betty, for this fine testimony on the stewardship of time and prayer. I see that our time is gone. I want to thank each panel member for the help he has been in directing our thoughts in this discussion of "What Is Stewardship?" I trust that each one present tonight will re-examine his own stewardship in the light of what has been brought out. Let's close by singing the first and third stanzas of "Trust, Try, and Prove Me."

(AUDIENCE will join in singing.)

(*Curtain*)

SCENE 3

SETTING: *In a booth at Barrymore's Restaurant. If possible, have very soft organ music as background. Bob and Nancy enter and take seats.*

NANCY: It's so nice of you to bring me here, Bob. The lights are lovely on that fountain, and I do enjoy the organ music.

BOB: So do I. (*Hums a bar with the organ.*) Listening to good music with my best girl makes this a double treat. (*Picks up menu card.*) What would you like to eat?

NANCY: You order for me.

BOB (*laughing*): Trusting, aren't you? How do you know I won't order snails or some other queer food? (NANCY *smiles;* BOB *looks at card.*) All right— if they ever get to us!

NANCY: I don't care if they don't. I enjoy just listening to the music and talking.

BOB: I keep thinking of what was said tonight. You know, I'm afraid that in God's sight I've been an embezzler. I can start setting things right by sending a tithe of my pay back to the church every month. But I can't get the rest of it out of my mind.

NANCY (*thoughtfully*): Maybe we aren't supposed to.

BOB: You feel that way too?

NANCY: What I heard tonight put the clinchers on what I've often heard Dad say, but wasn't sure I believed. Now I'm convinced it's so.

BOB: What was that?

NANCY: "You'll never miss anything worth while in life by letting God have all there is of you." And, Bob, it came to me tonight, as I sat there marveling at Betty Baker, that it must be this way: the more you let God have of you, the more you have of Him.

BOB: I guess that's right. (*He pauses.*) I especially like your Dad's statement. (*He repeats it as if saying it to himself.*) "You'll never miss anything worth while in life by letting God have all there is of you." (*He looks at* NANCY *and takes her hands in his across the table.*) Nancy, let's change it just a little. Let's say, "We'll never miss anything worth while in life by letting God have all there is of *us.*"

(*Curtain*)

WANTED—A FRIEND

Importance of Friendliness

CAST OF CHARACTERS

MAVIS, *a young woman*
SHIRLEY, *a young woman in wraps*
TOM, *a young man in wraps*
ETHEL, *a young woman in wraps*
JACK, *a young man in wraps*
VERNA, *a young woman in wraps*
RUTH, *a young woman in wraps*

SCENE: *Average living room. Shirley is reading a book as* MAVIS *enters.*

ఆ ఆ ఆ

MAVIS: Oh, Shirley, guess whom I saw today!

SHIRLEY: Judging from your excitement it must have been (*fill in a well-known personality's name*) or someone equally exciting or notable.

MAVIS: No one notable, but someone exciting; someone from home.

SHIRLEY: Well, that is exciting, anyone from Dearville would be a treat. Who was it, male or female?

MAVIS: Both, darling, it was Tom Wiles and Verna Paxton.

SHIRLEY: Not really! Where were they and what were they doing?

MAVIS: Standing on the corner of (*fill in with local streets*) having a reunion and powwow. They had just run into each other and were going through the do-you-remember-whens as I came out of (*local firm*) and bumped right into them. And they're coming over tonight and Tom said he thought maybe he could get hold of Jack Holmes and bring him along. He's going to school here. Verna thought maybe she could get hold of Ruth Doorman. She works out south. Have we anything we can use to make sandwiches? My goodness, they're apt to be here any minute now. I was *forever* getting home. A woman driver got crosswise of the street and stalled her engine. Did it snarl up traffic!

SHIRLEY: Gracious! There's the doorbell now. Let them in.

(*General greetings and handshakings, exclamations, questions about work, relatives, etc.*)

TOM: Say, do you remember that steak fry the Agoga class had?

ETHEL: You mean the Amoma class. We girls thought it up and invited you.

JACK: Well, we paid for the steak. I guess that made it our fry.

VERNA: Didn't we have the best times at the old Dearville church? Where do you folks go to Sunday school now?

(*Silence*)

SHIRLEY: Goodness, folks, don't you go anywhere? Why, what would Pastor Roberts think of you all! You ought to be ashamed!

TOM: Well, where do *you* go?

SHIRLEY: I—well—I—you see—I go to the (*fill in local name*) as much as anywhere.

RUTH: When did you last go?

SHIRLEY: What are you, a policeman? I guess it was Easter, if you must know the truth.

JACK: Say, what's the matter with this gang? We don't believe you can fall from grace, but this certainly sounds like an epidemic of backsliding. What's the matter?

SHIRLEY: I'll begin. The first Sunday after we got to the city I hunted up a church, and true to my training I went on time. I got there five minutes before time and there was hardly a soul around. Just the custodian and an old lady with a hearing aid were all. Eventually a few more came in and the department superintendent got up on the platform and apologized for no opening program.

VERNA: And we have such interesting ones at Dearville!

MAVIS: Yes, they always helped get you into the right frame of mind for Bible study. What did you find, Jack?

JACK: Something like it. I went to Sunday school when I first came and I nobly stuck it out there for more than a month. In all that time they never used anybody but teachers and officers in their programs.

They did a 100% job of leaving the pupils out—.

MAVIS: Talk about being left out! That was the way it was in a class I went to when I came here. The teacher did all the talking throughout the lesson period. There was never a chance for a pupil to participate in any way.

TOM: You can stand a teacher lecturing if he knows what he's lecturing about, but it's downright pitiful to sit in classes where the teacher consults his quarterly all the time. Back home they always said the Bible was the textbook of the Sunday school and that the quarterly was for home study.

RUTH: Listen, being *left* out is nothing compared with being *frozen* out. That's what happened to me. Nobody spoke to me when I went in, while I was there, or when I left, and I gave them plenty of opportunity to do so. I was lonesome!

TOM: I had calls, but they were the perfunctory, official kind.

MAVIS: I know what you mean. I used to just wish and wish some girls would ask me to go to prayer meeting with them, or meet them on my noon hour for lunch, or bring Mother some flowers. They knew she was sick because I asked prayer for her, but no one did anything.

SHIRLEY: That's right. We had office friends and boarding-house friends, but somehow there were no Sunday school friends, and they were the ones we needed most, especially when Mother died.

ETHEL: When Verna asked where we went to Sunday school, I was waiting for someone else to speak first. I'm the exception to this crowd. I was fortunate enough to find a congenial Sunday school, but it was probably because I knew people in it before I ever went there. I am so glad I did keep quiet and get the benefit of your remarks. We have a problem in our department over at (*name local church*). It is this: we had so many visitors—for instance, in August there were 29—but they never became members. I think you folks have told me some reasons why. I've tried to jot them down. Let's see if I have them all:

1. Poorly prepared and presented opening programs. That's where people get their first impressions, isn't it?
2. Lack of cordiality. It means a lot to a stranger to be warmly greeted.
3. Follow-up fellowship. This includes calls prompted by a genuine interest, not just a sense of duty. It also means personal companionship.
4. Sharing of responsibility. We all like to have a part.
5. Good Bible teaching. This means well-prepared teachers who actually teach because they've studied subject, method, and pupils.

JACK: And put a bracket around all five points, Ethel, and label them "Friendliness."

ETHEL: That's a good point, and you may be sure

I'm going to duly emphasize every point you have discussed, but now may I say a few words to you folks?

TOM: Shoot!

ETHEL: Before I came over here I was studying next Sunday's lesson on "The Cost of Being a Friend." One Scripture that comes to me is from Proverbs 18:24: "A man that hath friends must show himself friendly." Probably you all did that, but if you didn't, remember that is one of the first rules for the visitor to any Sunday School. Jesus Christ is the supreme example of friendliness. Then try to look upon everything with a kindly, not a critical, eye. Give them the benefit of the doubt. Recollect that after all, we weren't perfect back at Dearville church, we slipped up on a good many things, and we certainly slipped up in some very important things if so many of us, as soon as we leave, fall away from the Lord, and forsake His service. You know Jesus wasn't pleased with everything at the temple, but He always went there to worship. Forgive me, if I seem to preach, I don't mean to, but tomorrow is Sunday. Won't you all start out anew and go to Sunday school somewhere?

TOM: Yes, I will, and I'll go home tonight and study the lesson if you'll tell me where it is.

OTHERS: "Me too." "Sure."

SHIRLEY: That's fine. Now let's all go out to the kitchen and make some sandwiches.